ACKNOWLEDGEMENTS

These quotations were gathered lovingly but unscientifically over several years and/or were contributed by many friends or acquaintances. Some arrived—and survived in our files—on scraps of paper and may therefore be imperfectly worded or attributed. To the authors, contributors and original sources, our thanks, and where appropriate, our apologies. —The Editors

CREDITS

Compiled by M.H. Clark
Designed by Joanna Price

ISBN: 978-1-935414-00-1

1st Printing.
Printed with soy inks in China.

HELLO, WORLD!

Compiled by M.H. Clark ★ Designed by Joanna Price

COMPENDIUM™
INCORPORATED

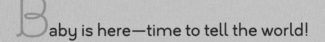

Baby is here—time to tell the world!

— — — — — —
unknown

Making the decision to have a child—it's momentous. It is to decide forever to have your heart go walking around outside your body.

- - - - - - - - -
elizabeth stone

Bringing a child into the world

is the greatest act of hope there is.

- - - - - - -
louise hart

Our children will create
a world we cannot imagine,
they will accomplish things
we cannot even dream.

- - - - - - - - -
kathryn t. shaw

There is nothing on earth like the moment of seeing one's first baby ... there is no height like this simple one.

katharine trevelyan

Birth is the sudden opening of a window, through which you look out upon a stupendous prospect. For what has happened? A miracle. You have exchanged nothing for the possibility of everything.

– – – – – – – – – – – – –
william macneile dixon

Having a baby can feel like winning the lottery, getting everything you wanted for Christmas, and falling in love all wrapped into one.

- - - - - - - - - -

jennifer louden

I knew the moment my child was born that
I was right where I was always meant to be.

- - - - - - - -
jenna higgins

Every child born into the world is a new thought of God, an ever fresh and radiant possibility.

_ _ _ _ _ _ _ _ _ _ _

kate douglas wiggin

A baby is love
made visible.

- - - - -

proverb

When you are drawing up your list of
life's miracles, you might place near the top
the first moment your baby smiles at you.

----
bob greene

A wee bit of heaven drifted down from above, a handful of happiness, a heart full of love.

helen steiner rice

Where did you come from, baby dear?
Out of the everywhere into the here.

- - - - - - - - - - -
george macdonald

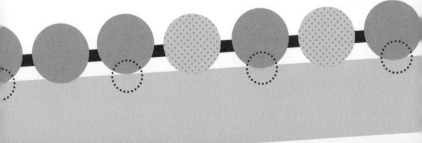

A mother's love is still the most powerful and mysterious energy in the world.

- - - - - - - - -
elizabeth david

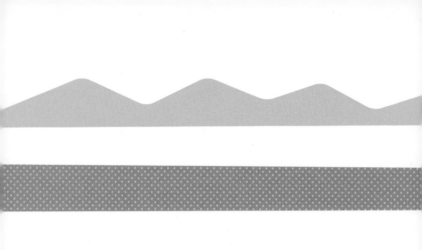

No man walks out of the delivery roo

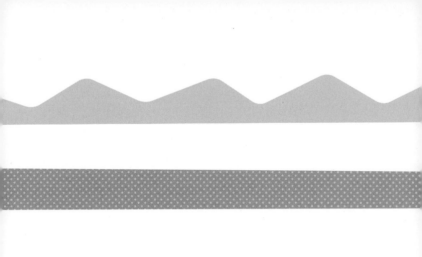

he same man who walked in.

- - - - - - - - - - - -
james douglas barron

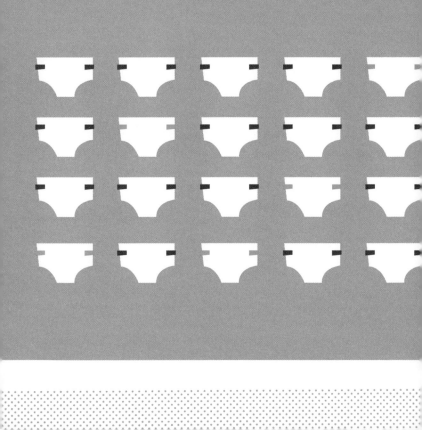

A baby will make love stronger, days shorter, nights longer, bankroll smaller, home happier, clothes shabbier, the past forgotten, and the future worth living for.

- - - - -
proverb

. . . One thing about having a baby is that each step of the way, you simply cannot imagine loving him any more than you already do, because you are bursting with love, loving as much as you are humanly capable of, and then you do; you love him even more.

– – – – – – –
anne lamott

Small child—once you were a
hope, a dream. Now you are reality.
Changing all that is to come.

– – – – – –
unknown

Parenthood is quite a long word.

I expect it contains the rest of my life.

- - - - - - - - - - - -
karen scott boates

How small. How beautiful.
Whatever happens in the years to
come, this is perfection. This is love.

– – – – – – –

pam brown